Author's Note

If you were to give up food and water for a whole day, you might get a feeling of what it's like for children and their families whose lives are so difficult that they don't have enough to eat.

If you were to do it every day for a month, you would also learn patience, gratitude, self-control, mindfulness and a sense of solidarity with everyone on the planet.

These are some of the reasons why Muslims fast during Ramadan. There are also spiritual reasons, such as strengthening our faith and our bond with Allah.

Not eating or drinking may seem hard, but when I was growing up in Malaysia, I couldn't wait to join in. Fasting is not compulsory for children, but many of us start practising at a young age. It took a lot of tries before I could fast the whole day, and when I did, I was amazed at what I could achieve.

When I moved abroad to study and work, I had a very different experience of Ramadan. Where I grew up, there was a festiveness and sense of community because everyone fasted together. In my new home, I often fasted alone. However, when I explain the reasons for fasting to my curious friends, I'm able to reflect on why it's so important to me.

You may find that you are fasting while the world carries on as normal. Or you may have a Muslim friend and would like to know more about Ramadan. Regardless of your faith, we can all embrace this special time in the year through sharing our stories and being kind to one another.

The Month of Ramadan

Inda Ahmad Zahri

Crocodile Books, USA
An imprint of Interlink Publishing Group, Inc.
www.interlinkbooks.com

To everyone who believed in me—
thank you. **I.A.Z.**

This month is **different** from the others.

It starts with the sighting of a new crescent moon.

Around the world, families, friends and neighbors wish each other,

"Ramadan

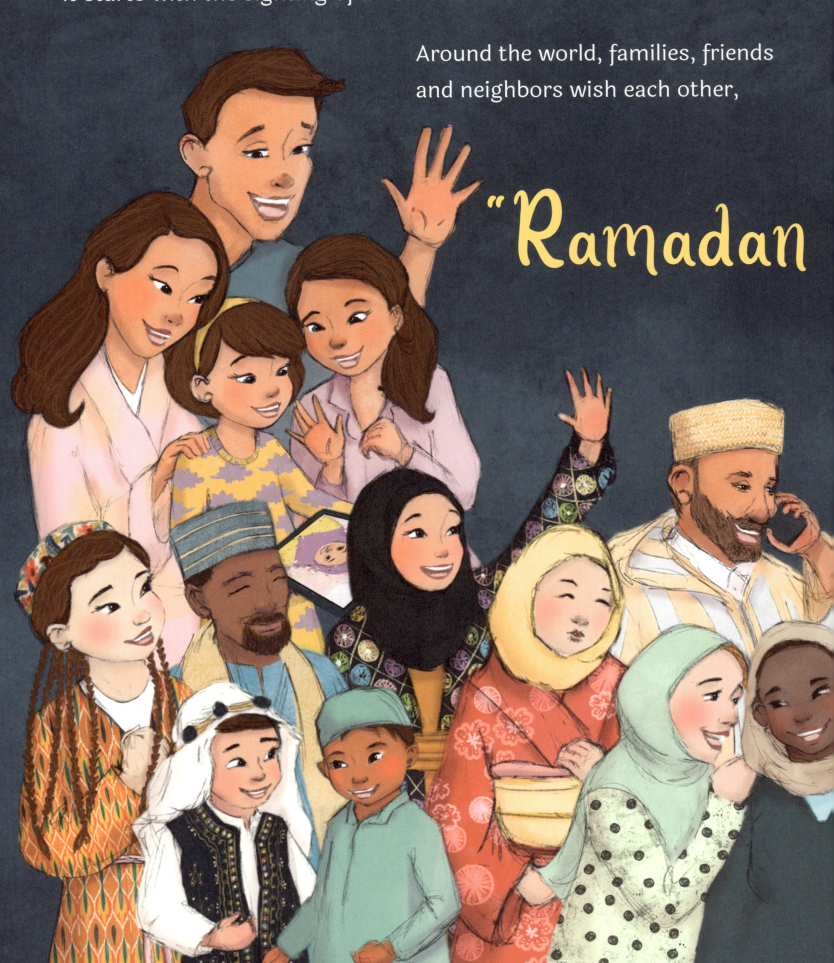

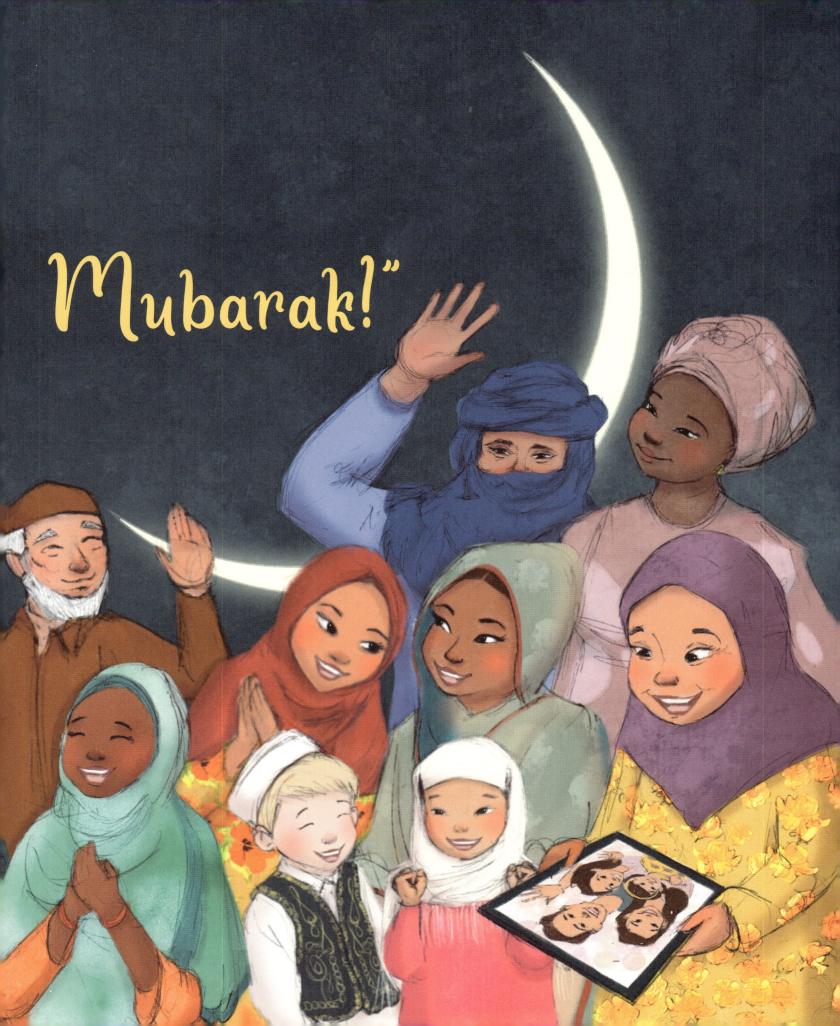

This month, we have breakfast before the sun comes up.
My eyes are still shut as tightly as the wings of a bird in its nest.

Mama puts a plate of dates on the table for **suhoor**.

"Here you go, Deenie," says my big sister Juju, picking out the shiniest ones for me. "These will give you energy for your first day of fasting."

Can I really manage without food and water until sunset?

Maybe if I were a **hibernating bear**...
but I can't sleep in a cave all day.

"It's hard," Mama nods, "especially for little ones.
But you can try it for a couple of hours if you like."

"Slow down, be **kind** to yourself and think **good** thoughts."

She pushes Papa's favorite snacks to the back of the
pantry along with a handful of our unwanted habits.

This month, we learn to do **big** things by changing one **little** thing at a time.

Each day, I last a little longer without eating and drinking, but my tummy still **rumbles** when lunch boxes snap open.

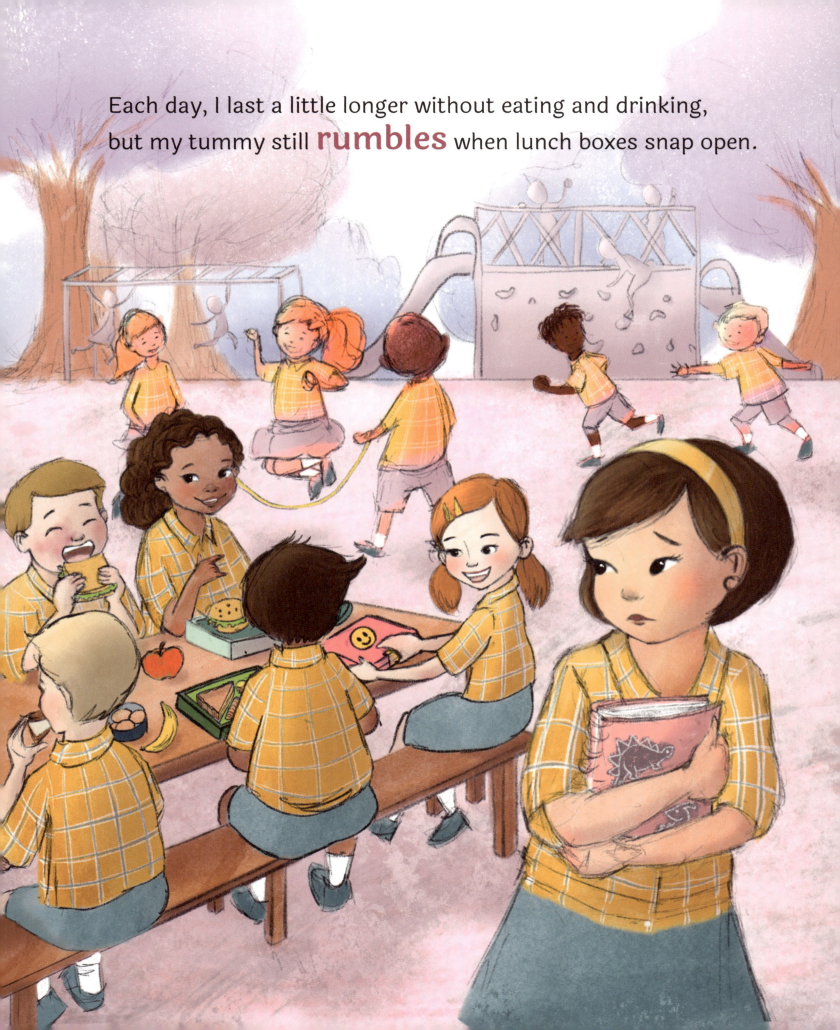

At first, I feel **lonely** in quiet spaces,

but soon I find slices of life
I would've otherwise missed.

This month, I join Coach on the bench instead
of scoring on the field.

It turns out I'm great at making game **plans**.

Juju gives up screen time and works on a cool science project.

Papa sets aside time to read and Mama prunes the garden,
pondering and **remembering**.

Our new habits grow like her roses
when our minds aren't rushing around.

Finally, I make it all the way to **iftaar!**
Cool water rushes down my throat.
Hot dishes smile up at me.

Juju and I are in heaven as we dig into our favorite food. Has it always tasted this good?

This month, the ordinary feels **extraordinary**.

Our mosque opens its arms wide
as we file in for **tarawih** prayers.

The **imam** recites **Quranic** verses he has learned by heart.

Mama winks at us when it's time to head home, but many others stay to pray longer. Mama says that some stay all night.

"Why, Mama?"

"Because it's a chance to look **inwards** and **upwards**."

Above us, the universe hums.

Inside of me, I feel **peaceful** and **strong**.

I feel I **belong**.

"Where I grew up, we had a food bazaar outside the mosque," Papa smiles.

He stops at a desk where families pay **sadaqah** and **zakat** to help those who spend most of the year hungry.

I remember how my tummy rumbled during the day.
I tug Papa's sleeve and slip my own coins into his palm.

This month teaches us to share with those who do not have much,
while reminding us to be **thankful** of how much we have.

Zakat / زكاة

The moon grows **fatter**.

Papa's clothes grow **looser**.

He drops them off when he and Juju volunteer at the relief center.

Juju helps with forms and letters,
and gets tips for her experiments.

Mama's friends catch up at a gallery so that
she won't miss out on their usual lunch dates.

"They really didn't need
to go out of their way,"
she says later at soccer
practice, but her cheeks
are pink with delight.

I feel strong enough to play today, so
Coach gives me a thumbs-up.

When I score, the team goes **WILD!**

Coach can't believe I'm still fasting . . . and neither can I!

"My body is **amazing!**" I say.
"So's your **mind**," says Coach.

"So's your **heart**,"
says Mama.

This month I see **kindness** everywhere.

Every **word**,

thought

and **gesture**

means something
to someone.

Another new crescent moon. Another round of wishes.

This time, we prepare new clothes, gifts, and food, and say,

"Eid Mubarak!"

"I'll miss Ramadan," I say to Mama, Papa and Juju.

Above us, the moon reminds us of everything we've learned.

Inside of me, something has grown **bigger** and **better** than ever before.

A month like this can make my **whole** year.

Glossary

Ramadan is the ninth month in the Islamic calendar. Muslims fast every day from dawn to sunset and are also encouraged to abstain from bad habits, bad words and bad deeds. You could say that it's like a month-long bootcamp for the soul!

Suhoor is a meal taken before dawn. Traditionally, this included dates, which were easily found in the Arab lands during the time of the Prophet Muhammad, and contains natural sugars and minerals. Dates are also commonly eaten for iftaar.

Iftaar is the breaking of fast at sunset. After a day without food, you may feel like gobbling up your dinner, but it's best not to overeat. Being moderate is also part of a healthy Ramadan!

Tarawih is a special prayer that is only held during Ramadan. Worshippers often complement the prayers with the recital of the Quran to strengthen their faith and remember their blessings.

Imam is a person who leads the congregation in prayer.

Sadaqah and **Zakat** are donations or alms. Sadaqah can be done voluntarily at any time, but Zakat is compulsory if you have the means to donate to the poor. This can be as little as the cost of two cups of grains.

Eid or Eid'ul Fitr is the well-earned celebration after a long month of fasting. Muslims visit each other, ask for forgiveness from each other, dine together and exchange gifts.

First American edition published in 2025 by

Crocodile Books
An imprint of Interlink Publishing Group, Inc.
46 Crosby Street
Northampton, Massachusetts 01060
www.interlinkbooks.com

Copyright © Inda Ahmad Zahri, 2023

First published in Australia in 2023 by Allen & Unwin

Library of Congress Cataloging-in-Publication Data available
ISBN 978-1-62371-618-9

Illustration technique: hand-drawn with Apple Pencil on iPad Pro using Procreate

Cover and text design by Jo Hunt
Set in 17 pt Laila Regular

10 9 8 7 6 5 4 3 2 1

Printed and bound in Korea

FSC
www.fsc.org
MIX
Paper | Supporting responsible forestry
FSC® C023083